This Book

Belongs To

....

....

Printed in Great Britain
by Amazon

39512543R00056